Revive Your Parenting

Revive Your Parenting
C.P.R. for Parents™

A Philosophy based on
Compassion, Patience, and Respect

Terry Manrique
Expert Parent Coach

Revive Your Parenting.

Written with the help of Germán Manrique and Jamie Strauss
Editing by Christina Cutting
Formatting by Rafael Manrique
Cover Design by Accelerator Advertising Inc.
Cover Photography by Magdalena Manrique

ISBN-13:978-0999478905 (Working With Parents, LLC)

ISBN-10:0999478907

Dedicated to My Wonderful Family

To my husband, Germán who has always supported me and most importantly always believed in me and my talent for working with children and their parents. This book would not have happened if it wasn't for him pushing me to believe in myself. Thank you, honey, for pushing me out of my comfort zone—it was worth it.

To my beautiful children, Marissa, Rafael and Magdalena, I hope I have made you proud. I am very blessed to have such wonderful and supportive children. Believe in your dreams, keep pushing forward, and make them come true.

Contents

Acknowledgements

I would like to acknowledge several people for their encouragement to create this book. I wish to thank all my clients for inviting me into their homes and allowing themselves to be vulnerable in front of this new stranger in hopes of finding a way to be the parent they were meant to be. Watching my clients, parents and children, transform in front of my eyes has been the biggest blessing and the most rewarding feeling anyone could have. Thank you for letting me experience that feeling with you. You all have asked time and time again for me to write a book to help you get even closer to being a better person, partner, and parent.

To my husband, Germán Manrique, thank you my love for the countless hours helping with my business. For the past 7 years you have advised me, given me direction, and helped set goals. Thank you also for all your hard work helping revise and edit the book and constantly encouraging me to complete it. Thanks for seeing all of my potential.

To my son Rafael Manrique, thank you for sharing your talents. You along with your father have provided countless hours of help in the past 7 years of business. From creating my logo, setting up my first website, and now formatting this book to make it look beautiful for my readers. Thank you son for being there for me. I love you and can't wait to do more extraordinary work with you!

A special thanks to Jamie Strauss who has been with me since I started my business. She has been the best partner anyone could ask for. Jamie helped me write blogs, newsletters, and collaborated with me on this book and is the co-author of our second book, Change Your Perspective, Improve Your Parenting. I've always said she is the other half of my brain. We have always been on the same page, and whenever I have an idea, she helps me complete it. Thanks Jamie for going on this journey with me.

About the Author

Hello, I'm Terry Manrique, your Expert Parent Coach. I am very honored that you are reading this book. I started my journey as a young 22-year-old mother of a toddler when I walked into a preschool classroom of 15 toddlers as an assistant preschool teacher. I quickly connected with the children and recognized their skills, personalities, and behaviors and naturally connected with them by providing structure, positive redirection, and compassion for their lack of verbal skills, patience for their struggles and exploration, and respect for their creations. At the time I was totally unaware that I was using the C.P.R. concepts.

Fast-forward after 7 years as an early childhood education teacher, working with children from toddlers to kindergarten, and then 10 more years working as Program Director helping teachers and parents identify and deal with different types of child behavior challenges, I was able to focus on observing those challenging behaviors, build the tools to deal with them, and implement various types of solutions to rectify them. I then leveraged that experience to start my own business as a Parent Coach to help families resolve behavioral challenges they were dealing with in their home.

My experience has allowed me to provide parents with a crash course in Early Childhood Development to help them better understand how their child thinks and be empathetic to what their child's needs are. Understanding your child and knowing WHY they behave the way they do can eliminate the frustration many parents face. Now I'm writing this book about the concepts I developed over the last 23 years.

Introduction

I'm just going to come out and say it. Parenting is hard. You are trying to raise competent, functional human beings; guide them in their decision making until they can make the right choices on their own. All the while, you are juggling schedules, planning and preparing meals, cleaning, tending to laundry, working, and caring for the health and needs of your family, pets, and yourself. You are stretched thin, stressed out, and sometimes it affects your parenting.

We've all been there. We've yelled a little too loud, a little too often. We've rolled our eyes, or heavily sighed at yet another question from our child. We've dismissed our child's feelings because we were in a hurry, or didn't want to make a scene. It happens to everyone at some point or another, but if it's happening more and more often, you may need to administer C.P.R. to your parenting.

I developed the C.P.R. philosophy over the past 23 years as the basis of my approach to creating and maintaining healthy parent/child relationships. C.P.R. can be applied to children of any age from infants to teens and even adults.

C is for compassion, P is for patience, and R is for respect. *Revive Your Parenting, C.P.R for Parents* is a guide you can use to resuscitate your relationship with your children. Over my career, I have refined the C.P.R. philosophy and applied it successfully in many situations. Working with both children and adults, I have learned that we are all looking for compassion, patience, and respect. These three basic components are at the core of basic human needs. Understanding their meaning, and learning how to incorporate the concepts behind C.P.R. into your interactions with your children, will help you to establish healthy and meaningful relationships with them. The relationships you have been longing for will start to develop. My hope is that by reading this book you will learn to apply these skills not only with your children but also in your relationships with others around you.

Parenting Today

Parenting has become a challenge with so many different rules, parenting styles, platforms, social media, mom groups, etc. Everyone is trying to be 'in the KNOW' and 'on top of their game' when it comes to raising their children. The world has changed so much, and there are so many distractions that demand our time and attention: smart devices, 24/7 work schedules, social media, gaming, and extracurricular activities, just to name a few.

Everything is at our fingertips, from quickly finding an answer to any question on your computer or phone, to making purchases at the push of a button. Instant gratification is what this world expects. This plays a big role in how the world has impacted us as parents; we are falling into the trap, and are expected to provide instant gratification to our children. Parents want to make their children happy and give them everything right away. Your children know this; as a result, you start to see your child expecting you to provide them instant gratification. It's hard to say no, and it's hard to stay focused with all the distractions, so you start down the spiral of always trying to please your kids, but you never fully reach that point, which causes you to continue going down the spiral even further. You are hoping that at some point you will satisfy your child's needs but when all is said and done, you end up raising a child that has unreasonable expectations and you find yourself at a point of no return.

During my work with families, I have discovered that most parents have no clue what direction to go, or whom to take advice from when it comes to their children. Constantly questioning themselves, they try method after method and then feel disappointed when they do not see instant improvement. They start to lose their confidence and feel increasingly overwhelmed. Finally, they realize that what they are doing isn't working for them or their child. Many families are having the same challenges, and when parents share their challenges with each other, it creates the assumption that the issues that they are dealing with are normal, acceptable, and have no solution. That does not have to be the case. When you apply C.P.R. you can feel strong and confident that you are now headed in the right direction with your children. You can raise them the way you have always wanted.

Most of my clients prefer not to parent like they were parented. They have similar responses when I ask them about their experience with their parents; they were spanked, misunderstood, not supported, not respected, not validated, or their parents were too strict. They often only remember the extremely negative aspects of how they were treated by their parents because it affected how it made them feel. They forgot what their parents did right; developing rules, consequences, discipline, and of course, ultimately providing love to them. It's true, parenting in those days was a bit extreme and harsh, but the end goal was to make sure children knew how to be good people when they grew up. The point is that you need both ways of parenting; the positive aspects of the old along with the new. That is what the C.P.R. philosophy is all about, establishing a delicate balance when it comes to Compassion, Patience, and Respect.

Understanding Your Child

Before we get started with the components of the C.P.R. philosophy, let's determine your child's temperament.

- Is your child strong willed? Is your child calling all the shots and running the household?
- Does your child have tantrums several times a day?
- Do you feel you are being bullied by your child?
- How long have you been dealing with these behaviors?
- One year, three years, seven years?

No matter the age, you still must show compassion to your child because the bottom line is that you are the parent that allowed this behavior to continue; unless, of course, your child has extreme behavioral challenges that have been diagnosed. (If that is the case, the C.P.R. philosophy can still provide you lots of great tools to implement, but please understand that support from other resources will be necessary.)

How do you know if your child has extreme behavioral challenges? This can be very confusing for many parents. The easiest and most effective way to understand if your child is controlling a situation, or truly has no control, is by assessing their behaviors in various environments such as school, parks, or in the homes of other family members or friends. If you hear from your child's teacher, family, or friends that they are also having similar challenges with your child's behavior, then that's a red flag to bring up to your pediatrician as the first step in a formal diagnosis or reach out to an Early Childhood Intervention Specialist for children 5 and under. However, if you are hearing from your child's teacher and your friends that your child is so wonderful and they love having them around, then you can be more confident that the unwanted behavior can be controlled and rectified by you. This, in fact, is a red flag for you as the parent that your child has learned to manipulate you. This is a sign that your child is in the driver's seat, and if the behavior is extreme, then they are ready to drive themselves and you off the cliff unless you take over.

No child should have that much control. It is extremely unhealthy for their development. This is also a heavy burden on the child, and that is why it's translating into challenging behaviors. The more control your child has over you, the more misbehaviors you will see. Children need and crave rules, structure, and discipline. They may not know this, but it's how they feel safe, loved, and challenged in a positive manner. The reason your child is acting out is that they are unconsciously looking for boundaries. So, how do you make the adjustments necessary to reverse the cycle and get the results you want? You start by challenging your child in a healthy and supportive way through Compassion, Patience, and Respect (C.P.R.).

This book will provide examples of how to use the C.P.R. philosophy during everyday challenges or issues with your children. You may already be implementing some of the concepts of the C.P.R. philosophy in your household. In that case, my hope is that this book will help validate your methods, provide you encouragement to continue the good work, and show you additional strategies.

Assess Your Child

1. What extreme behavioral challenges is your child exhibiting?

2. Does your child exhibit these behaviors when you or your partner is not around in various environments such as school, parks, or the homes of other family members or friends?

Yes / No

Ask your child's teacher, family or friends about your child's temperament. If you are hearing from those other sources that your child is so wonderful and they love having them around, then you can be confident that it is a behavior that can be controlled and rectified by you. This, in fact, is a red flag for you as the parent that your child has learned to manipulate you.

Develop a Behavior Management Plan

Every parent should have a behavior management plan. Sit down with your partner and talk about the behaviors you want to see from your child/children. Being on the same page as parents helps with sticking together and following through. Plus, you avoid "good cop" versus "bad cop" parenting with your children. You stay united.

1. What are the behaviors you want more of?

2. What are the behaviors you want less of?

3. What are the behaviors you will not tolerate?

The next section will provide strategies to encourage desirable behaviors and discourage unwanted ones.

Compassion

Let's start with the first component, Compassion. When we have compassion, we try to understand a situation or issue from the other person's point of view. When you demonstrate compassion, you show others that you are concerned about their struggles. Children need to feel your compassion and know that you understand their struggles following rules, accepting consequences, and being disciplined. The unfortunate truth of most parental compassion is that parents don't know how to balance the amount of compassion that they provide along with the discipline children need. Many times, parents take compassion to the extreme by over sympathizing (or catering to their child's misfortunes and sufferings), which many times leads your child to believe that they can get away with bad behavior again, or that someone else will be accountable for their actions.

Children need to learn from their mistakes and have consequences first, to understand expectations, and then, to feel the accomplishment of overcoming behavioral obstacles to meet expectations successfully. When you eliminate the consequences for them, you are essentially robbing your child of the chance to learn from their mistakes.

As a parent, it's your job to always play that role, even when it's difficult, heartbreaking, or painful. Showing compassion will help you, and your child, during a moment where you need to stick by the rules or follow through on the consequences. During certain situations emotions can run high while parenting. You are dealing with not only your own emotions but also with the big, over-the-top emotions of your child. When you're in the midst of a situation with your child, it is important that you leave your emotions out of it, focus on the reason you are in the situation, and understand this is a teachable moment. Understand that children are very intuitive, and can read your emotions and energy fairly quickly, so work on keeping your emotions under control. An example of how easily your children pick up on your emotions would be the first time you leave them with a caregiver. Your anxiety of leaving them for the first time is usually emulated by your child. If you are nervous, anxious, or upset, your child will see that and take it as a cue that they should also feel nervous, anxious or upset. However, if you leave the house with smiles (even if you actually are upset), then your child will feed off your positive emotions and be more at ease. Basically, we need to keep our emotions in check so we can be compassionate and understanding of our children's emotions.

Parenting is not easy, and there will be times when it will feel easier to just give in to avoid immediate stress for you or your child. However, giving in doesn't teach them to learn from their mistakes. Here are a few different examples of how to balance showing compassion while standing strong, and not sending mixed signals.

Following through with a consequence for bad behavior:

Child: "Mom, I don't understand why I can't play with my friend today."

Parent: "Max, I'm very sorry you can't go play with your friends today. You must be very disappointed about this, and I understand that. However, we talked about the consequence, and you continued with your behavior, so <u>YOU</u> decided not to play with your friends. Next time you will have the chance to make a better choice."

This example would be for a child age 5 and up. You clearly show an understanding of how your child may be feeling, but you are also reiterating the fact that your child is in the situation because of a choice that he made. You are also reminding him that he will have a chance in the future to make better choices. You are being firm, while also showing compassion for his current feelings.

When your child has no choice in the situation:

Parent: "Max, I need you to please get your shoes on; we need to go run errands."

Child: "I don't want to run errands! That's SO BORING!! I just want to stay here and play."

Parent: "I understand that errands are boring for you. Sometimes they are boring for me too. There are definitely other things that

I would rather be doing than running errands, but they need to get done."

Child: "But I just want to stay here and play!"

Parent: "I know, but the quicker we go get our errands done, the quicker we can get back here to play. I'm sorry, but this is something we just have to do, and you do not have a choice. But if you are cooperative, we can get done faster."

This example is also appropriate for children 5 and up. Nobody really enjoys running errands, and when you communicate to your child that you understand his feelings about the subject (and maybe that you feel the same way), you then can move towards getting through the situation. For a younger child who doesn't have a choice in the situation (whether going to run errands or being buckled into their car seat), you will have to use more direct statements rather than reasoning.

When a younger child has no choice in the situation:

Parent: "I understand you don't want to do this/don't

like this, but this is what we are doing/what needs to happen. When we are done going grocery shopping and you do a good job listening to me, then when we get home you can play with that special toy you like or we can make your favorite snack."

These are just some examples of how you can be firm while demonstrating compassion. As you maintain consistent but firm compassion, your child will recognize that.

Again, show an understanding and acknowledgment of their feelings, but be very clear about what will be happening now. Many young children just want to have a choice in what is happening to them, or knowing what is happening next to be part of the plans. So if you understand this, and assure them that they can make choices afterward, or be part of the planning process, then they will usually be compliant.

When presenting your child with two appropriate choices, resulting in you making the choice:

Parent: "Sam, do you want to wear your sweater or

this long sleeve shirt today?"

Child: "I want to wear my swimsuit!"

Parent: "I understand you really want to wear your swimsuit, it's beautiful, but it's winter, so it's not an option today. You can choose your sweater or this long-sleeved shirt."

Child: "I want to wear my swimsuit!"

Parent: "I'm sorry, but that is not a choice today. You can choose one of these two, or if you can't make a decision, I will choose for you."

It is at this point that you allow your child to mull it over for a short time, and then tell her she had her chance to make the choice, so you are now making it for her. She may throw a tantrum because of the choice you have made, but be calm and compassionate, reminding her that by not making a choice she decided to let you decide. Assure her that she will be able to have another chance to decide another time.

When presenting your child with two appropriate choices, resulting in your child getting nothing:

Parent: "Sam, would you like grapes or an apple for your snack?"

Child: "I want candy!"

Parent: "I understand that you love candy, but that is not a choice. You can choose grapes, an apple, or you can choose nothing."

Child: "I want candy!"

Parent: "Sam, this is your last warning. You can have an apple or grapes. If you can't decide, then I guess you're not hungry, and there will be no snack. Do you understand? The choice is up to you."

You can use this example for children 2 years and up or earlier if they are communicating or if they are starting to challenge you. You are showing compassion for her love for candy, but also stating that candy is not an appropriate choice. By allowing choices for snack in the first place, you are showing her that you understand her need for some independence and decision making. If your child doesn't make an appropriate choice, then you have to stick with the consequence until the next mealtime or snack time, not five minutes later when they decide they are ready to make a choice. They may have a tantrum after you follow through and another when they ask again, but it's important to stay the course and show them compassion about the choice that they made. They can choose to make a better choice next time, but this is the consequence for now.

It's also important to make eye contact and be at their eye level when you are having these kinds of conversations. Really listen to your child by getting rid of all distractions (turn off the television, put down your phone or tablet, pull over and park). Let them express how they feel, and acknowledge their feelings, but stay the course and don't give in. Explain to them that they will get another chance to try again and make better choices. By getting down to their eye level and really listening to their feelings, you are demonstrating that you sympathize with what they are experiencing; this is the ultimate form of compassion. Not only are you demonstrating how to properly show compassion to someone, but you are show-ing them you understand and validate their feelings. And when a child feels understood and heard, they are less likely to throw tantrums, and more likely to be receptive to what you are saying.

Compassion is truly the game changer in how quickly you will get results. Your child can feel from you the compassion you have for them and how it's all for their own good. This displays love, safety, and an under-standing of your role as the parent. It allows you to be the authority figure and keeps you from losing control. When you can understand this concept, then implementing consequences won't feel so bad for you and for your child because they will come to learn that you are doing your job with love and compassion for their feelings. They will come to respect you even more and feel safer in their environment.

Compassion Review

Think of past situations where you had to implement a consequence for bad behavior.

1. What consequences have you used in the past?

2. Are you seeing results from your consequences?

Yes / No

3. Are you having a hard time coming up with consequences?
   If so, why?

4. How do you think you can apply compassion when it comes to consequences?

What are some steps you need to take to help you develop compassion and follow through with consequences while curbing the guilt that you feel for temporarily upsetting your child?

5. How do you feel when you set and uphold consequences with your child? Do you feel guilty?

6. What is holding you back from setting and upholding the consequences?

7. What are some steps you need to take to help you develop and model compassion and follow through with administering the consequences necessary to hold your child accountable for their actions?

Start understanding that this is not about you and it's your job to be the parent, be there for your child, and be concerned about their well-being. Remind yourself that your child needs you to teach them to learn from their mistakes and apply compassion while doing so. They need consequences to know where the limits are.

Patience

Patience is a virtue. We've all heard it, and I'm sure we've all said it once or twice, but sometimes it is hard to put into practice. In this section, we will work with both you and your child when it comes to developing your patience skills. We will talk about how to control your emotions so you can be patient and compassionate with your child during stressful and challenging events like tantrums, meltdowns, screaming, or any other behaviors exhibited by your child when they lose control of their emotions. Finally, we will talk about how we can help our children to become patient individuals.

Building Parents' Patience

Patience is a skill that requires practice. Many adults have short tempers or minimal coping skills. If you are this person, I recommend that you practice meditation, recite mantras, or learn breathing techniques. Sometimes there are outside factors in our lives that affect our demeanor. Take a minute to sit down and reflect on your life to understand what is causing you to be so impatient. Is it your current job? Your marriage? Your lifestyle? Your environment? Start keeping a log of when you lose your temper and replay the situation in your mind when you are alone. Ask yourself how you would have done things differently and how you could have controlled your temper. When did you start to feel upset, angry, or like you were losing control of your emotions? Was there a specific trigger that made you lose control? This self-assessment skill is extremely important to model for your children; your children are a true reflection of yourself. If you find yourself behaving a certain way, check to see how your children are responding. They usually copy and implement the same behaviors they see from you.

Teaching Patience

Patience is a skill that is learned early on in life, and one of the main questions parents ask is, "At what age can I start teaching my child to be patient?" You can start as early as 8 months. Next, parents often ask, "How do I teach my child patience?" Here are a few ways to teach your child to practice patience.

Techniques for parents to use with their child:

- Have your child wait a few seconds before you give them their snack, juice, or whatever they are asking for.
- If you are in the middle of a task when your child is asking for something, tell them you will attend to their needs after you have completed the task.
- Teach your child to do things for themselves rather than jumping to fulfill every request.
- Teach your child to ask politely instead of giving demands.
- Do not act on getting them anything until they are able to communicate correctly.
    - Asking kindly by saying "Please."
    - Without whining, screaming, or yelling

— Not bossing you around.

The key to implementing positive behaviors regarding patience is to be constantly aware of these 5 examples and address them accordingly. How you behave with others in front of your child directly correlates to how your child will behave with you. Here are some unconscious parent behaviors that you need to be aware of:

Parental behaviors that your child may mimic unintentionally:

- Demanding that you get what you want right away from your spouse.
- Being impatient whenever you are in line at a store, and talking poorly about the person working there.
- Yelling at the other drivers when stuck in traffic.
- Being aggressive with your server at a restaurant because your food is taking too long, there was a mistake with your order, or other minor issues.
- The way you speak to your spouse/partner.
- The way you speak to your kids/family.
- Speaking badly about others when they are not around.

When children see these behaviors being exhibited by

you (their primary role model), they will think that the behaviors are acceptable.

Techniques for parents to model how to be patient:

- Talk things out with friends and family.
- Really be fair about the situation if you are wrong, acknowledge it and apologize.
- Be proactive by letting your child know what is going to happen before you react.
- Allow your child to have a chance to make a choice.
- Give your child the chance to figure things out on their own.

Assessing Your Child's Impatience

Use the following methods to help you understand why a child loses their temper and has a meltdown or a tantrum.

- Try to understand what happened to your child before they got upset.
- Evaluate the situation and be observant of what's happening around them. Many times, children lose their temper/emotions because they are being misunderstood, not acknowledged, or having a hard time

communicating with you.

- Don't always be in a hurry to fix the problem or to react in a negative way.
- Really take the time to understand what's going on before you react.
- Guide your child through this transition by helping them to relax before trying to solve the problem.

Steps to Improve Patience

1. Walk your child through the conflict step-by-step, so they understand what is happening, and why they are getting so emotionally upset.
2. Once you have an idea of what's happening, break it down for your child, so they can evaluate the situation themselves, and help your child take a different approach to resolve the problem.
3. There are many proactive ways you can prevent a child from having a tantrum or meltdown in the first place.

Learn to observe the situation first before overreacting and recognize when you are not taking notice of the situation. When you are not fully in the moment.

Working with over 500 children over the course of 23 years, I have noticed that the main reason children have tantrums or meltdown is that they are misunderstood. Communication is the biggest challenge for both the child and parents. There is so much, as parents, that we do wrong that causes our children to be frustrated. Here are a few things that frustrate your children and cause them to have emotional outbursts.

Parent behaviors that cause children to feel misunderstood

- You underestimate their abilities.
- You cater to them too long.
- You hold them back by not allowing them the opportunities to learn from their mistakes.
- You assume they don't know better.
- You do things for them because it's faster and easier.
- You don't have the patience to show them how to do it themselves.

I am sure at some point someone exhibited at least a few of these frustrating behaviors with you. Try to remember how that made you feel. Did you feel frustrated, angry, or incompetent? No one ever wants to be held back, limited or denied of their potential. When we are treated in this way, sometimes it brings out the worst in ourselves. Your children don't have adequate practice expressing themselves, so having meltdowns or tantrums is the only way they know how to communicate their feeling. It isn't until you as the parent takes time to guide them and help them express how they feel that things begin to change.

Patience with Infants and Toddlers

Being patient with our infants is easier for many because we know they rely on us for everything. They are not to blame and have no fault of their own. Doing everything for your baby for one full year is a long time, and you become programmed that way. However, once your child turns 8 months or so, the game starts to change a little bit. Yes, of course your child needs you for everything still, but they are also starting to be much more aware of their body and their world. This means it's time for them to explore even more. Remember before when they were confined to a small space and limited in where they could be? Now they are rolling, army crawling/crawling, walking, and getting stronger both physically and mentally. Suddenly they are not infants anymore! They are crossing a new milestone into toddlerhood, and what a great thing that is for them when we, as the parents, understand what this means.

When you practice patience with your little ones, you will see great results for both you and your child. Believe it or not, you can apply these techniques with your infant as young as 6 to 8 months old when they first start exploring the world around them.

Exploration and Redirecting

Have you ever noticed how your children never really play with their toys but are much more interested in the household items around them? How they prefer to crawl and grab/touch the non-toy items? I am sure you know exactly what I am talking about. Think about that situation for a while and play with that scenario in your head. Here's an example, imagine your 7-month-old infant army crawling to where you have your shoes or dog food. They are immediately attracted to these items and want to explore them by grabbing these items and putting them in their mouth. What is your first reaction? What goes through your head? As a parent, your first automatic reaction may be to pick the child up and move them away from the area. You react this way for one main reason, SAFETY. Which I agree with, as long as you are near your child and can make sure they are safe. However, this is a great opportunity to start redirecting your child to make better choices and listen to you when you redirect them. Redirecting your child is not an easy task, and requires lots of patience on your part. Your child is determined to explore and will try again and again to grab those items until they have learned what you expect from them and you will need to continue to redirect them over and over again. That is the only way to make a breakthrough with your child.

Eventually, your child will start to understand what they can touch and play with, and what they are not allowed to play with or touch. It starts with you being consistent and patient with yourself. Ultimately, you are the one who needs to practice this to get results. You are the one who sets the tone, who sets the rules, who sets the expectation. The way your child behaves or does not behave is in your hands. Having the proper techniques and following through is key to understanding and having a successful relationship with your child.

Redirecting your child to make better choices is not easy. It will require time and patience and may need to be repeated several times before it starts to sink in. Of course, changing any behavior is going to be difficult, but you will see results if you follow the C.P.R. philosophy. Eventually, children learn from their mistakes and realize what it is that you expect from them. They will learn to control their emotions and work through different situations. If you apply these strategies consistently, your child will learn to evaluate their choices aware of the resulting consequences. The goal is for your child to learn to think things through, and ultimately make better choices. Teaching your child these methods as early as 8 months will benefit them as they grow from toddlerhood to their teenage years and beyond. However, the person you are training the most is you, the parent, to be consistent and patient when it comes to helping your child correct or redirect their behaviors. And of course, you should expect to get pushback from your child because they are going to feel compelled to see how far they can push the limits.

If you take the time to try this technique with your 8-month-old child while they are exploring their environment, you will notice one of two responses from them:

1. Your child will get upset quickly when you just pick them up and remove them from exploring, causing them to have a meltdown or tantrum.
2. Your child will continue to insist on exploring and will return to what they want until they figure out this is not for them to explore or touch. Eventually, they will start to pass up the item and just move on to the next adventure.

Soon enough they will start to understand boundaries. Just make sure you allow them space to explore and yourself the time and space to address the behaviors. As long as they are exploring in a safe environment, it's okay. For example, if they head for the shoes and dog food, you can redirect the child by just slightly moving them away from the items while reinforcing appropriate behavior with patience and kind words such as: "Max, the dog food is not for you. It's for the dog," or "Yucky! Shoes are dirty and not for playing with." After several attempts, your child will understand and move on to the next exploring opportunity. Notice how the word NO was never mentioned in those sentences. Using the word NO is an impatient shortcut, used to avoid explaining why the child should not do the behavior. So remove that word from your vocabulary. Not only does this keep your child from learning the word NO, but it will enhance your child's vocabulary as well. Back to exploring. They might move on to play with the kitchen cabinet and the plastic bowls inside and it's okay for you to have a cabinet or two for your child to explore. "Yes, Max, you can play with that. Have fun exploring." Before you know it, Max will bypass the shoes or dog food and go straight to the cabinet to explore. If you are patient and consistent, you and your child will succeed in communicating effectively.

This is when your child starts to learn to trust your word. Mean what you say, and say what you mean every single time and your child will know exactly what you expect from them. When you take the time to teach this valuable technique early on, you'll be amazed how well your child will listen to you during their preschool years and beyond.

Encouraging Independence

As your child grows, so will their desire for independence. They will want to do things more and more on their own, and they will want to help you with tasks as well. In these situations, you will need more of a planned patience, rather than just controlling your emotions sort of patience. What do I mean? Imagine you have a doctor's appointment at 10 a.m., so you know you need to leave your house at 9:30 a.m. You also know that your toddler has become insistent on putting on his own shoes. Plan for this by telling him to get his shoes on well before 9:30 a.m. If at 9:25 a.m., when you slip your shoes on, you tell him to get his on, and the minutes begin to tick by as he fumbles with the tongue, the straps, and pulling the heel on properly, then having to take it off because it was the wrong foot ... What is happening now? You are becoming anxious because you need to leave, so you just put his shoes on for him, but now he is upset and crying because you robbed him of the opportunity of accomplishing his task. This could have all been avoided if you just gave him a little more time to accomplish the task himself. Toddlers are learning to do many new things, so they are going to be (painstakingly) slow at each task until they master it. The catch is that they won't be able to master a task if they can't practice, so you need to allot extra time in your schedule so that you are able to remain patient.

This sort of planning ahead can be applied to tasks they are helping you with as well. For example, if you are baking cookies or cooking dinner, and your child wants to help you, know going into it that they will extend the prep and cleanup time. They are still just learning how to measure and pour properly, how to crack an egg and mix ingredients in a bowl without flinging it everywhere. By accessing the situation before you let them help, you will be prepared to be much more patient with them, and they will learn from and enjoy the experience so much more. However, if you know you are on a tight time schedule, maybe politely refuse their help for that day, but promise to make more time for them to help another time; there is no need to create a stressful situation if you don't have to.

If you are teaching your child to clean, you need to realize that they will not clean perfectly at first, and you may have to go back and do it again. A few ideal chores for toddlers are window/mirror washing (using a spray bottle of water and a cloth), sweeping, using a dust buster, wiping down counters and tables, and dusting with a duster or dusting mitt. You will need to have the patience to walk around with them, coach them on how to properly clean, give small demonstrations, and then let them do their best. Their best won't be awesome, and you'll probably have to go back and do it yourself, but they are learning and growing their independence. One thing to keep in mind is to not lose your patience and just take over the task; this will either cause your child frustration that will come out as yelling/crying/tantrum, or it will just discourage them from attempting the task again. And if you do need to go back over their work, try to wait until they are not around, or respectfully point out where they went wrong, and demonstrate to them how they could have done better. "Oh, I see you really tried hard at this task! Nice work. But I see a spot you missed. Can I show you how to check for missed spots?" This sort of patience will encourage their learning and development while also showing respect for the efforts they have already put forth.

Patience Review

Start keeping a log of when you lose your temper and replay the situation in your mind when you are alone. This self-assessment log is extremely important and helpful to see if your children are imitating your behaviors. Include the following in your log:

1. Describe the situation that made you lose your patience. What happened?

2. When did you start to feel upset, angry, or emotional?

3. Was there a specific trigger that tipped you over the edge?

4. How could you have done things differently?

5. How could you have controlled your temper?

Techniques you can use with your child to develop patience

1. When do you start to address poor behaviors? Are you being pro-active or reactive?

2. What techniques can you implement to become more patient? Be specific.

3. What do you do if you are in the middle of a task and your child wants something from you?

4. What can you do to start making things easier for your child to become independent so they can do things for themselves instead of asking you for everything?

5. What are some things you can do to help your child wait a few seconds before jumping to their needs?

Behaviors your child mimics from you unintentionally

Take the time to think about things you see your child doing that they have learned from you. Make a list and talk it over with your partner. How is this affecting your partner as well? Be open to having a conversation to help each other improve on your weaknesses and build on your strengths. Be honest, truthful, and vulnerable. →

Parent 1   **Parent 2**

Respect

The final component of the C.P.R. philosophy is respect. Showing compassion and being patient are ways to show respect. In this section, I want to make it clear how important it is to develop respect for everyone in the household. In the past, the focus was on respecting your elders, but not very much was said about respecting the child. I know it has been made very clear to modern parents that we have done a 180-degree turn on this idea, and we now focus on making sure the child is heard and paid attention to. However, we are still unbalanced in both; there is not enough respect for parents in some instances and not enough respect for children in others. Respect should be given to everyone, young and old; however, you can't expect to be respected if you are not giving respect to others, your children included. It appears we are forgetting this, allowing our children to disrespect us completely, and missing the whole point of respect altogether.

Respect for Parents

It's important for your children to respect you, as you are showing them respect as well, but most importantly, as you are showing respect for yourself. Bullying is a hot topic in many communities. Many parents don't realize how much they are getting bullied at home by their own children. This happens when you don't respect yourself enough to put a stop to it. I know you may disagree with me, and say you do have respect for yourself, but would you ever let anyone else speak to you or yell at you the way your children do? NO! Yet, you allow your children to disrespect you every day, and you tell yourself that one day they will grow out of it. Fast forward years later, and your children are still disrespecting you. You love your children, but you don't like them. You know your children are not bad; they have just developed bad habits that you didn't put a stop to and which have ended up shaping them. This was no one's fault, you just didn't know better; you were doing the best you could with what you knew. You had the best intentions and wanted the best for your children, except the techniques you used backfired on you, and you don't know how to turn things around.

So the first step is respecting yourself. Set limits, rules, and consequences, stick with them, make sure your partner agrees with them and sticks to them as well, and make sure your child knows that you will not tolerate being disrespected. It is important that you and your partner are always on the same page because there is nothing more frustrating than being led by two leaders that are going in different directions. Being misled over and over can cause anyone to feel angry and unhappy. This is where consistency is key. Once you start to remain consistent with what you both say, your children will see that you are sticking to your word, respecting yourself, and they will begin to respect you and your rules as well. Consistency takes practice and is dependent on your own personal mood on a particular day, but it is important to practice it.

How easy is it for you to respect someone who is always changing their mind based on how they feel that day? Imagine going to work and not knowing what you are going to walk into that day because your boss is so inconsistent. His view of you and your coworkers are based on how he feels. If he is in a good mood then nothing will go wrong, but if he is in a bad mood, everything goes wrong, and everything is wrong, and everyone is doing everything wrong. This kind of leadership is unhealthy and can bring out the worst in you. It is toxic and is one of the main causes of an unhappy work environment. It's also difficult to respect bosses that favor some employees more than others based on their personality, their looks or their manipulative ways. This kind of favoritism causes animosity within the work setting. Not only do you not respect your boss, but you also lose respect for the favored co-workers. When there is favoritism in the home, your children develop animosity towards each other, and the last thing you want for your family is for your children to develop this kind of relationship with one another.

Modeling Respect

In what other ways can you demonstrate respect in order to teach your children how to show respect? You can demonstrate by giving respect to everyone you interact with on a daily basis. Whether it be a server at a nice restaurant, the person working the drive-thru window, the cashier at the grocery store, the teachers at your child's school, or the customer service representatives you are speaking to on the phone, they all deserve respect. When you treat people you interact with respectfully on a regular basis, you help your child to see that it is the correct way to interact with others. How do you think children learn to talk down to people or to be dismissive of other's feelings? They learn from watching you and how you respond to situations. Remember, you are their first and primary role model since birth.

In today's world of social media, we've been seeing a lot of shameful displays of disrespect towards those in the service industry. You've seen the viral videos with some person who feels like they are better than the worker for one reason or another, yelling and screaming, demanding that their issue be resolved immediately, and throwing insults at the staff. We watch these videos and cringe because we know this is unacceptable, but imagine that instead of watching a video, you are a child watching your parent act this way. Children learn from their parents' actions, and when they see their parents mistreating others, they learn to deal with problems in the same way. However, if you are consistently polite with people, calmly and patiently requesting an issue be rectified, then THAT is what your child will learn, and that is how they will treat you when they are 5, 15, 25, or 50.

Finally, you need to show respect in your own home. And while this is probably one of the most important places to display respect, it is often the most easily overlooked. What do I mean by that? We spend our days at work, at school, out in public, being polite and respectful, and when everyone comes home; our family tends to get the worst side of ourselves. We are tired, crabby, emotionally and mentally worn down by the end of the day, and this may cause us to be short-tempered with our family members. However, it is of the utmost importance that we demonstrate, through our own words and actions, that no matter how we are feeling, we need to show respect to those we love.

What does this look like? Does this mean you have to be happy all the time? No. Respect doesn't equate to a cheerful mood, it just means that you will always treat your family members, children, and even pets, with respect. Always look your children in the eyes, and give them your full attention when they want to speak to you. If you are occupied or just need a moment, let them know, "I cannot wait to hear what you have to say, but let me finish with this, and then I can give you my full attention." Nothing screams respect for your child more than focused personal attention to their thoughts. When telling your children to complete a task for you, always use please and thank you.

"Max, I need you to hang up your coat and back-pack, please."

He does.

"Thank you."

Even if you get to the point where you've asked seven times already, don't yell and scream, go straight up to them, look them in the eye, and then say in a calm yet stern voice, "Max, I have asked you several times to hang up your coat and backpack, and they are still sitting on the floor. This needs to be done now." In this case, please is not necessary. If they are not getting up, you can now walk them over to the site of their task, and thank them

when they are done. Do you see how this was authorita-
tive while still being respectful? Now what if your child is
throwing a tantrum when you walk over to them because
they refuse to go on their own? You simply wait until they
are ready to cooperate with you. You do not let them do
anything else until they have completed that task at
hand. So no TV watching, no playing with their toys,
no interaction whatsoever. Eventually, your child will be
bored and will cooperate with you.

You can also demonstrate respect for your children
by honoring their boundaries. They don't want a hug or
kiss, that's fine, maybe later. They don't want to share a
particular toy with a sibling, OK, that is their decision
with their toy. Of course, some toys, communal toys, must
be shared by all, but help your child talk things out and
figure out which toys are sharing musts, and which ones
are sharing optional. If your child is scared or saddened
by something, don't just dismiss their feelings about it.
You should remove them from the situation that scares/
saddens them, and talk about why they feel that way, and
what you can do to help make them feel more at ease.
Sometimes we like to tease each other in our family, but
when we notice that one of our children is becoming
angry or sad about it, we respect their emotional bound-

aries and stop immediately. We then reassure them that we love them, we were only playing around, and we are sorry that we hurt their feelings.

We are sorry that we hurt their feelings. That is important. As parents, one of the biggest ways we can show our children respect is to own up to and apologize for our mistakes. Notice how I didn't say, "I'm sorry your feelings were hurt." That sort of apology doesn't take ownership of your mistake. When you acknowledge your own wrongdoing, it sends three messages to your child: first, that you, their parent, can and will sometimes make mistakes; second, it is important to own your mistakes; and third, it tells them that your apology is sincere. Not only does apologizing demonstrate your respect for your family, but it also builds up your credibility. Now your children know that what you say or do is the right thing, and if it is not, you will admit it and apologize for your mistake.

Finally, always showing respect for your partner. Again, use please and thank you when asking them to do something for you. Do things to help one another out on a daily basis. Praise them when they do something that helped you out. When you argue, do so in a respectful manner. Try not to raise your voice, and never resort to name-calling or personal attacks; keep the argument about the issue at hand. It is OK, even healthy, to have civilized arguments in front of your children; it will further demonstrate what a respectful argument and proper conflict resolution look like. Never speak badly about your partner in front of, or to, your children. This goes for married and separated parenting partners alike. Children should grow up learning that both of their parents deserve respect, and no one should undermine that. Remember, you can be angry with your partner, but if you don't have anything nice to say, it's best if you don't say anything at all.

Respect Review

1. Make a list of things your children are doing now that are disre-
spectful toward you or others.

2. What steps can you take to start earning respect from your children?

Once you have your list start addressing the behavior by asking your
child to try again with a kind manner or different tone. Model for
them what it should look like or sound like so they know what you are
expecting and be aware of how you are reacting in similar situations.

3. How will you demonstrate respect in order to teach your children how to show respect?

4. How do you think you can apply compassion when it comes to consequences?

Putting it All Together

The truth is that your kids deserve the best, without a doubt. The problem is, knowing how to help them succeed through our own actions and choices. I am hoping you have learned from the previous sections how balancing firm boundaries alongside compassion, patience, and respect can lead to positive results from your children.

The truth is that your kids deserve the best, without a doubt. The problem is, knowing how to help them succeed through our own actions and choices. I am hoping you have learned from the previous sections how balancing firm boundaries alongside compassion, patience, and respect can lead to positive results from your children.

The Importance of Observation

- How do you start to recognize what is happening in your household? Observe your children. What is really going on? Who is in control?

- In what areas has your child taken the lead, and what are the techniques they have learned to manipulate their environment? Start writing down behaviors that are happening before and after a meltdown, or a challenging situation. How you are behaving in these situations?

- Are you losing control of the situation? Of yourself? Of your emotions? Are you having an adult tantrum in front of your child?

- Are you setting the example that you are losing control and allowing them the power to control your emotions?

- Are you watching what is happening and listening to their needs?

- Are you so stressed out that you can't even focus on what's in front of you?

- Are you feeling defeated when challenges arise?

- Do find yourself walking away because you don't have the proper tools to deal with situations?

Take ownership of your own actions.

Recognizing the problem is the first step to creating a plan for change. Your children are not responsible for driving the bus. In fact, many of them are close to driving over the cliff if you don't take the wheel. Your children are literally crying for help and acting out to get your attention to take over and take control. Your child is desperately looking for you to guide them in the right direction. No one ever wants to feel out of control, and your child is telling you just that. Your child has learned, at a very early age that if you don't take control of a situation, they can and sometimes must. They have also learned how far they need to go to get what they want before you break or give up. What parents don't understand is that a child's job is to cross the line and figure things out through trial-and-error. This is part of their natural development, but your child will never learn how far they have gone and they will continue to push even more when you don't set boundaries. We would never let them walk off the cliff's edge, yet this is exactly what you are doing when you don't take control and address issues right away. You need to step in and take control of the situation to guide them through it. It's your job as the boss/leader/parent to train your child how to discern between right and wrong. When you take the time to train your employees, you develop loyal, respectful, and happy people, which translates to an overall positive work environment. It takes time, patience, and consistency to see results. The same concepts apply to parenting. The hardest part of parenting is learning from our own experiences when we were growing up. We forget that someone had to teach us to be respectful, polite, and kind. We forget that someone had to take the time to discipline us. We take so much for granted because these things just start to come naturally to us over the years. You were not born knowing how to behave, communicate, or express your feelings, and neither was your child.

Recognize how you are also manipulating things when it's convenient for you.

- Why do parents put a shield over their eyes?
- Why are we so quick to recognize how smart our kids are when they are doing the right things, but make excuses when they misbehave?
- Why can they understand us when we are playing, but not when we need them to behave or listen?
- Why do we have a hard time understanding that they

do know what's right and wrong?

- Why do we take the time to teach them how to play a sport, but not teach them how to cooperate with us?

Again, we don't want to see our children suffer, or be unhappy, and therefore we don't set the rules or the expectations to correct the misbehaviors because we know doing so would make them unhappy.

You need to recognize that everything is a game to your child. They want to win the game of wills. Between you and your child, who has the most willpower to get through a challenge? Remember this is not intentional; it's how they work things out through trial-and-error. For example, a parent with an infant will play all these cute games while the child is fully interacting with them and understanding the game, but when the infant throws their toy, and we say, "That's not nice," the child does it again to see what will happen. Then, the parent picks up the toy and hands it to them. And again the child will throw it then the same routine repeats itself several times. The child has learned how to control the parent, and the parent thinks they don't understand. Who won this game?

The more you recognize what's happening in your household, the more insight you will get—and the more you will be aware of what's happening and why. You will also start to understand the importance of being consistent for the sake of your child and yourself. And when you recognize that you are the one that needs to make the changes and implement corrective measures, you can quickly start to see positive results. Your children are waiting desperately for you to be their leader and the hero.

Parent of Pre-Teen to Teens

How do you deal with children at this age? Is it too late?
No! It's not too late, but it's going to be extremely challenging. There will be a lot of resistance and name calling
from your kids. It really depends on the overall relationship you have with them. Most importantly, if you are
raising your child with a partner, grandparent or other
family member, it is extremely important that you are
on the same page with the C.P.R. Philosophy and your
approach.

If there is zero respect, then it will take a great deal
of will power and dedication on your end. Everyone wants
to feel loved and accepted so you can approach your new
changes from that perspective and be very vulnerable.

Parents: "We are sorry we haven't done our job correctly as parents when you were younger,
but things have to change for all of us.
We love you so much that we can't allow
this behavior to continue so here are some
things that are going to change starting
today."

If you have an okay relationship with some amount of respect you can sit down with your child and say:

Parents: "We are sorry we haven't done our job correctly as parents when you were younger, but things have to change for all of us. We love you so much that we can't allow this behavior to continue. Let's talk about some of the things that need to change."

Now if you have a pre-teen make sure you start talking about the give and take relationship. Make them aware that they can't continue to just take, take, take all the time and continue with their poor behavior. You need to put a stop to the bad habits and make your child more accountable for their actions. Let them know that if they don't correct the identified behaviors that you can't continue to give them what they want. You need to have them understand that at this time they cannot make it on their own in the real world without your help and they will need to start earning all of their "wants." Tell them that you will provide their basic "needs" but that is it. Yes, that means no extracurricular activities if they cost money, no shopping for extra clothes, no spending money, etc. Think about the give and take concept during this time of restructuring the relationship and the level of mutual respect that needs to be earned. When you see your child make positive changes let them know you are okay with providing them the cash to go out or you are willing to buy those jeans they worked hard to earn throughout the past weeks. This does not mean that the process is done. Evaluate the continuing behaviors and provide the "rewards" accordingly. If they are not making the efforts to improve their behavior, you simply explain how sorry you are that they haven't made any changes in their behavior and you therefore cannot provide them with the cash to buy those jeans or give them money to go out.

Remember why it's important to set boundaries as soon as possible, because it's much harder to set these limits when they become young adults. Once your child hits the age of 16 they can pretty much be on their own. They are exposed to so much more and can be easily influenced by their peers to make risky decisions. They can be more independent because they can get a job, drive a car, or spend more time away from home. Repairing your relationship with your child is the highest priority and needs immediate attention. Depending how extreme your situation is, I encourage you to seek out professional help to get the proper guidance and support.

Apply the Framework

Here is the framework to implement the C.P.R. philosophy with your child.

1. Recognize that you are a big part of the reason your child's behavior is out of control.
2. Understand that you don't know what you don't know, and that's okay. So, don't beat yourself up for what has happened in the past; learn and move forward with confidence. You can only control what you do now and plan for the future.
3. Explain to your child that change is going to happen because there is no other choice. It may be difficult, but it is what is going to happen because it's what's best for everyone.
4. Be strong, be consistent, be confident in the role you have with your child.
5. Now take the lead, set boundaries, rules, and administer consequences.
6. Finally, stay the course! Don't give up and don't give in!

After reading through the C.P.R. philosophy, I hope you now understand how you can start making the changes needed. Take the time to sit down with your partner and think about the changes that need to be made by both of you and your children. Start keeping a log of the behaviors you would like to work on and make the time to address them with your children with Compassion, Patience, and Respect. Recognize that you are the reason your child developed most of these bad habits, and recognize what you need to do to make the changes as well. Change is hard for everyone, but it's going to be harder for you as the parent to implement and reinforce what is needed to start seeing positive behaviors. The age of your child will determine how challenging it will be to make the changes. They will fight for the power to keep things the way they are; however, if they see you use the C.P.R. philosophy to stay calm and in control of your emotions, they will come around and appreciate your new parenting techniques, but it will take dedication on your part. I wish I could tell you that it will take a day, a week, or a month. The main way to ensure success is to faithfully implement the C.P.R. philosophy every time. Once you start to see some changes the improvements will quickly be evident.

In my second book, Change Your Perspective, Improve Your Parenting, Jamie Strauss and I will provide more in-depth guidance and tools to help you create positive changes for you and your family. I look forward to sharing more techniques and proven practices from my experiences helping families to make positive changes. Keep in mind this book is not meant for you to read it once, but to come back and refer to the information as you require ongoing support. I would love to hear about your challenges and your success stories and hear about what steps you took to create positive changes for you and your family. If you are still having difficulty, I am here to provide expert parent coaching services via phone, Facetime, Skype or in the home. Feel free to contact me by email at info@ourparentcoach.com and feel free to check out my website at www.ourparentcoach.com to download the worksheets for free.

Final Recap

- Start recognizing what is happening in your household.

- Observe your children. What is really going on and who is in control?

- Take control of your emotions.

- Make sure you plan ahead of time with your partner when you are going to start making drastic changes.

- Do your homework before addressing all the challenges you want to change and make sure you both are on the same page.

- Stay in the C.P.R. mindset.

- Start addressing the behaviors and act on them. Don't ignore them anymore. By not addressing the behavior you are sending a clear message that it's okay.

- Change is never easy for anyone, but change does take time and patience.

- Plan for your first day to be incredibly tough. Your child is going to fight you to keep control and that's okay and all part of the process.

- Just be there for them, keep your cool, and think C.P.R.

- If you apply the C.P.R. philosophy correctly, you will see changes within a few days.

- It's also very normal for you to see your child starting to challenge you again after 2 weeks of good behavior. Be strong and stay the course, they are just testing the limits.

- If you are not seeing any results within 2 weeks, take time to reassess the challenges you are facing, your reactions, and confirm that you are being consistent with your expectations and following through with your consequences.

- Finally, allow yourself at least 21 days of practice to fully let this concept sink in.

Working with Parents, LLC
www.ourparentcoach.com
info@ourparentcoach.com

Stay connected follow us on:
Facebook: @workingwithparents
Instagram: terryparentcoach

Be Strong, Be Consistent, Be Confident, and Be the Parent!

Made in the USA
Columbia, SC
20 November 2017